The Two 2011 NATO-led Military Operations in Libya

Copyright Page

TITLE: The Two 2011 NATO-led Military Operations in Libya

1ST Edition

Copyright @ 2023

Roberto M. Rodriguez. All rights reserved.

ISBN: 9798223184898

Table of Contents

The Two 2011 NATO-led Operations in Libya

By Roberto Miguel Rodriguez

Chapter 1: Operations Odyssey Down and Unified Protector: The Two 2011 NATO-led Military Operations in Libya

Background on the Libyan Crisis

The Libyan Crisis, also known as the Libyan Civil War, refers to the period of political unrest and armed conflict that took place in Libya from 2011 onwards. This subchapter aims to provide historians with a comprehensive overview of the events leading up to the crisis, setting the stage for the two NATO-led military operations in Libya.

The origins of the Libyan Crisis can be traced back to the authoritarian rule of Colonel Muammar Gaddafi, who had been in power since 1969. Gaddafi's regime was marked by repression, corruption, and a lack of political freedoms, leading to widespread discontent among the Libyan population. Inspired by the wave of pro-democracy protests sweeping across the Arab world during the Arab Spring, Libyans took to the streets in February 2011, demanding political reforms and an end to Gaddafi's rule.

The protests quickly escalated into a full-blown armed conflict, with anti-government rebels forming the National Transitional Council (NTC) to challenge Gaddafi's forces. As the conflict intensified, the situation on the ground became increasingly complex, with various factions, tribal rivalries, and regional power struggles coming into play.

The international community, particularly NATO, became involved in the crisis due to concerns over the humanitarian situation and the potential threat posed by Gaddafi's regime. The first NATO-led military operation, Operation Odyssey Dawn, was launched in March 2011 with the aim of enforcing a no-fly zone and protecting civilians from Gaddafi's forces. This operation transitioned into Operation Unified Protector, which expanded the scope to include the protection of civilians on the ground and the enforcement of an arms embargo.

The political motivations behind NATO's intervention in Libya were multifaceted. While the humanitarian aspect was emphasized, there were also geopolitical considerations at play, such as safeguarding regional stability and protecting oil interests. The legal and ethical implications of the interventions have been subject to debate, with some arguing that NATO exceeded its mandate and others highlighting the need to prevent a potential massacre in the city of Benghazi.

The impact of the military operations on regional stability in North Africa cannot be understated. The power vacuum created by Gaddafi's ousting led to increased instability in Libya and the wider region, with the rise of armed militias, the proliferation of weapons, and the spread of extremism. This has had far-reaching consequences, including the escalation of conflicts in neighboring countries, such as Mali and the Sahel region.

In terms of the effectiveness of the international coalition in achieving its objectives, there have been mixed results. While the military operations succeeded in protecting civilians and ultimately leading to Gaddafi's downfall, the subsequent lack of a comprehensive post-conflict stabilization plan has hampered Libya's transition to democracy and allowed for the resurgence of violence.

This subchapter will delve into all these aspects, providing an in-depth analysis of the Libyan Crisis and its ramifications. By examining the role of intelligence, air power, the United Nations, and post-conflict reconstruction efforts, historians will gain a comprehensive understanding of the complexities surrounding the NATO-led military operations in Libya and the enduring challenges faced by the country in the aftermath of the crisis.

Introduction to Operations Odyssey Down and Unified Protector

The subchapter "Introduction to Operations Odyssey Down and Unified Protector" provides a comprehensive overview of the two NATO-led military operations conducted in Libya in 2011. This chapter aims to provide historians and individuals interested in the niche of military operations in Libya with a foundational understanding of the events, motivations, outcomes, and implications of these operations. This subchapter sets the stage for the subsequent analysis and evaluation of various aspects related to these military interventions.

The chapter begins by introducing the two operations, Operations Odyssey Down and Unified Protector, highlighting their significance in the context of the Libyan conflict. It outlines the main objectives and strategic goals of each operation, emphasizing the role of intelligence in shaping the decision-making process and operational planning.

The political motivations behind NATO's involvement in Libya are explored, shedding light on the underlying factors that led to the military interventions. The chapter examines the legal and ethical implications of these interventions, considering the justifications put forth by the international coalition and the controversy surrounding the use of force.

Furthermore, the subchapter delves into the humanitarian aspects of the interventions, evaluating the effectiveness of the international coalition in protecting civilians and mitigating the humanitarian crisis. It also analyzes the impact of the military operations on regional stability in North Africa, considering the short-term and long-term consequences for the region.

The role of air power in Operations Odyssey Down and Unified Protector is examined, providing insights into the strategic use of air assets and its impact on the overall success of the operations. A comparison of the strategic goals and outcomes of the two operations further enhances the understanding of their similarities and differences.

The subchapter also addresses the role of the United Nations in supporting and coordinating the military operations, highlighting the challenges and achievements in this regard. The post-conflict reconstruction efforts in Libya following the interventions are also examined, shedding light on the challenges faced and the lessons learned for future interventions.

In conclusion, this subchapter serves as a comprehensive introduction to Operations Odyssey Down and Unified Protector, providing a solid foundation for the subsequent analysis of the different aspects related to these NATO-led military operations in Libya. It aims to provide historians and niche audiences with a holistic understanding of the events, motivations, and implications of these operations.

Objectives and Scope of the Book

The book "From Odyssey to Protector: Unraveling the Two NATO-led Military Operations in Libya" delves into the intricacies of the two significant NATO-led military operations in Libya, namely Operations Odyssey Down and Unified Protector. Addressed primarily to historians and individuals interested in the niches of military operations, intelligence, political motivations, humanitarian aspects, regional stability, air power, strategic goals, legal and ethical implications, international coalition effectiveness, United Nations involvement, and post-conflict reconstruction efforts in Libya, this subchapter aims to provide a comprehensive overview of the book's objectives and scope.

The primary objective of this book is to unravel the complexities and shed light on the multifaceted nature of the two NATO-led military operations in Libya. By analyzing various aspects, such as the role of intelligence, political motivations, and humanitarian considerations, the book aims to provide a holistic understanding of these operations.

The scope of the book encompasses a wide range of topics, including an in-depth analysis of the political motivations behind NATO-led military operations in Libya. It explores the factors that influenced the decision-making process and the underlying strategic goals of the international coalition involved.

Furthermore, the book evaluates the humanitarian aspects of the interventions, examining the impact on civilian populations and the efforts made to protect them. It also discusses the legal and ethical implications of these interventions, addressing questions of sovereignty, international law, and the responsibility to protect.

Additionally, the book examines the role of air power in Operations Odyssey Down and Unified Protector, analyzing the strategies employed and their effectiveness. It also compares the strategic goals and outcomes of the two military operations, highlighting similarities, differences, and lessons learned.

The impact of these military operations on regional stability in North Africa is another key area of focus. The book examines the consequences on neighboring countries and the broader implications for regional security.

Moreover, the study delves into the role of the United Nations in supporting and coordinating the military operations in Libya. It analyzes the effectiveness of the international coalition in achieving its objectives and the challenges faced during the intervention.

Finally, the book explores the post-conflict reconstruction efforts in Libya following the NATO-led military interventions. It assesses the successes, failures, and ongoing challenges in rebuilding the nation and establishing a stable and prosperous future.

In conclusion, "From Odyssey to Protector: Unraveling the Two NATO-led Military Operations in Libya" provides a comprehensive analysis of the objectives and scope of the book. By delving into various aspects, it aims to provide historians and individuals interested in military operations with a comprehensive understanding of the complexities surrounding these interventions.

Chapter 2: Role of Intelligence in Operations Odyssey Down and Unified Protector

Importance of Intelligence in Military Operations

The Importance of Intelligence in Military Operations

In the realm of military operations, intelligence plays a pivotal role in shaping the outcome and success of missions. This subchapter delves into the significance of intelligence in the context of the two NATO-led military operations in Libya, namely Operations Odyssey Down and Unified Protector. Addressed to historians and enthusiasts of military history, this section aims to shed light on the crucial role intelligence played in shaping the course of these operations.

Intelligence serves as the cornerstone of military planning and decision-making. It provides commanders with critical information about enemy capabilities, intentions, and vulnerabilities. In the case of the NATO-led interventions in Libya, intelligence played a pivotal role in identifying and assessing the targets, as well as monitoring enemy movements and activities. This enabled the coalition forces to effectively neutralize threats and minimize collateral damage.

An analysis of the political motivations behind these military operations in Libya is also crucial in understanding the intelligence aspect. Intelligence agencies' assessments and reports often inform policymakers about the potential risks and benefits of intervention, helping them make informed decisions. The accuracy and reliability of the intelligence provided to policymakers are instrumental in shaping their objectives and strategies.

Furthermore, the humanitarian aspects of the interventions in Libya cannot be overlooked. Intelligence played a critical role in identifying and targeting sites where civilians were at risk, thus aiding in the protection of innocent lives. It also helped in coordinating humanitarian efforts and ensuring the safe passage of aid convoys.

The impact of military operations on regional stability in North Africa is another significant aspect covered in this subchapter. Intelligence gathering and analysis helped in assessing the potential consequences of these operations on neighboring countries and contributed to contingency planning. It allowed the coalition forces to anticipate and mitigate any security threats that might arise as a result of the interventions.

The role of air power in both Operations Odyssey Down and Unified Protector is also examined. Intelligence enabled the effective utilization of air assets, providing valuable information about enemy air defenses and identifying high-value targets. This intelligence-driven approach allowed for precise and targeted airstrikes, minimizing civilian casualties and collateral damage.

Finally, this subchapter evaluates the effectiveness of the international coalition in achieving its objectives in Libya, with a focus on the role of intelligence. It also explores the legal and ethical implications of the interventions, analyzing the extent to which intelligence influenced the decision-making process within the coalition.

In conclusion, intelligence played a vital role in the two NATO-led military operations in Libya. It informed decision-makers, shaped strategies, identified targets, protected civilians, and contributed to the overall success of the missions. Understanding the importance of intelligence in these operations is crucial for historians and military enthusiasts alike, as it provides valuable insights into the complexities and dynamics of modern warfare.

Gathering and Utilization of Intelligence in Operations Odyssey Down

The subchapter titled "Gathering and Utilization of Intelligence in Operations Odyssey Down" delves into the crucial role of intelligence in the NATO-led military operation in Libya in 2011. This chapter aims to provide historians and enthusiasts of military operations with a comprehensive analysis of the intelligence gathering process and its utilization in the context of Operations Odyssey Down.

Intelligence played a pivotal role in the success of Operations Odyssey Down, enabling NATO forces to make informed decisions and effectively carry out their mission. The chapter explores the methods employed by NATO member states and their intelligence agencies to collect information on the ground, including human intelligence, signals intelligence, and imagery intelligence. It delves into the challenges faced in gathering accurate and timely intelligence in a complex and dynamic environment like Libya.

Furthermore, the subchapter examines the utilization of intelligence in planning and executing military operations. It highlights the importance of intelligence in identifying key targets, assessing enemy capabilities, and minimizing collateral damage. The chapter also explores the coordination between intelligence agencies and military forces, emphasizing the need for effective communication and the sharing of information to achieve operational objectives.

In addition to discussing the practical aspects of intelligence gathering and utilization, the subchapter also addresses the ethical and legal implications of these activities. It analyzes the principles of proportionality and distinction, exploring how intelligence can help mitigate civilian casualties and ensure compliance with international humanitarian law.

Moreover, this chapter provides a critical examination of the effectiveness of intelligence in achieving the strategic goals of Operations Odyssey Down. It evaluates the impact of intelligence on the overall success of the operation, including its contribution to the protection of civilian populations and the removal of the Gaddafi regime.

Overall, the subchapter on "Gathering and Utilization of Intelligence in Operations Odyssey Down" offers a comprehensive analysis of the role of intelligence in the NATO-led military operation in Libya. It caters to historians and those interested in the specific niches of military operations, intelligence gathering, and the political motivations behind the intervention in Libya. By providing an in-depth examination of this topic, it contributes to the broader understanding of the complexities and challenges inherent in modern military operations.

Gathering and Utilization of Intelligence in Unified Protector

In the subchapter "Gathering and Utilization of Intelligence in Unified Protector," we delve into the crucial role of intelligence in the NATO-led military operation in Libya. This section aims to provide historians and those interested in Operations Odyssey Down and Unified Protector with a comprehensive analysis of the intelligence gathering process and its impact on the outcome of the mission.

Intelligence played a pivotal role in both Operations Odyssey Down and Unified Protector, providing strategic and tactical information that guided decision-making processes. In Unified Protector, intelligence agencies from NATO member states and partner countries worked collaboratively to gather, analyze, and disseminate vital information on the ground situation in Libya. This intelligence helped shape the overall strategy and operational plans of the international coalition.

The collection of intelligence in Unified Protector involved various methods, including human intelligence, signals intelligence, and imagery intelligence. Human intelligence, gathered through contacts on the ground and covert operations, provided valuable insights into the intentions and capabilities of the Libyan regime. Signals intelligence involved intercepting and analyzing electronic communications, enabling the coalition forces to monitor enemy movements and communication networks. Imagery intelligence, obtained through satellite imagery and aerial surveillance, allowed for a detailed understanding of the military infrastructure and the location of potential targets.

The utilization of intelligence in Unified Protector was multi-faceted. It provided critical information for target selection, allowing the coalition forces to identify key military assets and infrastructure linked to the Libyan regime's ability to carry out attacks against the civilian population. Furthermore, intelligence played a vital role in minimizing collateral damage, as it enabled the identification of non-combatants and civilian infrastructure to avoid unintended casualties.

However, challenges and limitations existed in the gathering and utilization of intelligence. The fluid and complex nature of the conflict in Libya, coupled with the lack of reliable sources on the ground, posed significant challenges to intelligence agencies. Additionally, the political motivations behind the military intervention influenced the collection and dissemination of intelligence, raising questions about its objectivity and accuracy.

This subchapter aims to provide an in-depth analysis of the intelligence gathering and utilization process in Unified Protector, exploring its successes, limitations, and impact on the overall mission. By examining the role of intelligence in the military operation, historians and researchers can gain a comprehensive understanding of the complexities and dynamics involved in these NATO-led interventions in Libya.

Chapter 3: Analysis of the Political Motivations behind NATO-led Military Operations in Libya

Historical Context of Libyan Politics

The historical context of Libyan politics provides crucial insights into the two NATO-led military operations in Libya in 2011. Understanding the political landscape of Libya is essential for historians seeking to unravel the complexities of Operations Odyssey Down and Unified Protector.

Libya's political history is marked by a series of authoritarian regimes, with Muammar Gaddafi's rule being the most prominent. Gaddafi came to power in a military coup in 1969 and established a dictatorial regime that lasted for over four decades. His rule was characterized by repression, human rights abuses, and a disregard for democratic principles.

The political motivations behind the NATO-led military operations in Libya were rooted in the Arab Spring uprising that swept across the region in 2011. Inspired by the wave of protests calling for democratic reforms, the Libyan people rose against Gaddafi's oppressive regime. NATO's intervention aimed to protect civilians and support the opposition forces seeking to overthrow Gaddafi.

Intelligence played a crucial role in both operations. It provided valuable information about Gaddafi's military capabilities, locations of strategic targets, and potential threats to civilians. The intelligence gathered by NATO and its coalition partners enabled them to plan and execute effective military operations.

The humanitarian aspects of the interventions in Libya cannot be overlooked. While the primary objective was to protect civilians, the military operations inadvertently caused civilian casualties and infrastructure damage. Historians must evaluate the effectiveness of the interventions in achieving their humanitarian goals.

The impact of the military operations on regional stability in North Africa is another important aspect to consider. The power vacuum created after Gaddafi's fall led to a proliferation of armed groups and ongoing conflicts, particularly in neighboring countries like Mali and Tunisia. Historians must analyze the long-term consequences of the interventions on regional stability.

Air power played a crucial role in both operations. NATO's air campaign targeted Gaddafi's military infrastructure, weakening his forces and providing support to the opposition. Historians should examine the strategic goals and outcomes of the two operations to assess the effectiveness of air power in achieving the intended objectives.

The legal and ethical implications of the interventions in Libya are subjects of debate. Historians must analyze the compliance of the military operations with international law and assess the moral justifications for intervention.

The effectiveness of the international coalition in achieving its objectives in Libya is another area of interest. Historians should evaluate the coordination and cooperation among NATO member states and their partners in supporting the Libyan opposition and ultimately ousting Gaddafi.

The United Nations played a significant role in supporting and coordinating the military operations in Libya. Its resolutions provided the legal framework for intervention and facilitated international cooperation. Historians should study the UN's involvement and its impact on the success of the operations.

Finally, the post-conflict reconstruction efforts in Libya deserve thorough examination. Historians should assess the challenges faced in rebuilding the country and analyze the effectiveness of international support in achieving long-term stability and development.

In conclusion, the historical context of Libyan politics provides a comprehensive framework for understanding the two NATO-led military operations in Libya. Historians must delve into the intricacies of the political motivations, role of intelligence, humanitarian aspects, regional stability, air power, strategic goals, legal and ethical implications, effectiveness of the international coalition, UN's role, and post-conflict reconstruction efforts to unravel the complexities of these interventions.

Factors Leading to the NATO Interventions

The NATO-led military interventions in Libya, known as Operations Odyssey Down and Unified Protector, were complex undertakings with numerous factors contributing to their initiation. Understanding these factors is crucial for historians seeking to analyze and evaluate these operations, their motivations, outcomes, and implications. This subchapter aims to delve into the factors that led to these interventions, shedding light on the decision-making processes and the broader context at play.

One significant factor that precipitated NATO's involvement in Libya was the deteriorating humanitarian situation on the ground. The regime of Muammar Gaddafi had responded to widespread protests and demands for political reforms with brutal force, leading to a humanitarian crisis characterized by large-scale violence and displacement. This created a moral imperative for the international community, including NATO, to intervene and protect civilian lives.

Another factor was the political motivation behind the interventions. The Arab Spring had swept across the region, and the international community was keen to support popular uprisings and movements for democratic change. Libya presented an opportunity to demonstrate solidarity with the people's aspirations for freedom and democracy. Moreover, there were geopolitical interests at stake, such as securing access to Libya's oil reserves and preventing the country from descending into chaos, which could have had destabilizing effects on the region.

The role of intelligence played a crucial part in shaping the NATO interventions. Intelligence reports provided evidence of the Gaddafi regime's human rights abuses, its use of military force against civilians, and the potential for mass atrocities. This information informed the decision-making process and garnered international support for intervention.

The legal and ethical implications of the interventions cannot be overlooked. NATO's actions were justified based on the responsibility to protect (R2P) doctrine, which asserts that states have a responsibility to protect their populations from mass atrocities and that the international community has a responsibility to intervene when states fail to do so. However, questions were raised about the extent of NATO's mandate and the potential for mission creep.

Furthermore, the role of the United Nations in supporting and coordinating the military operations in Libya was instrumental. The UN Security Council passed Resolution 1973, which authorized the use of force to protect civilians, creating a legal framework for NATO's interventions. This resolution also provided a platform for international collaboration and legitimacy.

In conclusion, the factors leading to the NATO interventions in Libya were multifaceted. The deteriorating humanitarian situation, political motivations, intelligence reports, legal justifications, and the role of the

United Nations all played significant roles in shaping these operations. Understanding these factors is essential for historians seeking to analyze and evaluate the interventions, their outcomes, and their broader implications for regional stability, international cooperation, and post-conflict reconstruction in Libya.

Examination of Political Motivations in Operations Odyssey Down

The subchapter titled "Examination of Political Motivations in Operations Odyssey Down" delves into the intricate and multifaceted political motivations that shaped the NATO-led military operation in Libya in 2011. This subchapter aims to provide historians with a comprehensive analysis of the political factors that influenced the decision-making processes and objectives of the international coalition during Operation Odyssey Down.

Operation Odyssey Down was launched in response to the deteriorating security situation in Libya, with the aim of protecting civilian lives and preventing further violence. However, behind this humanitarian facade, there were various political motivations at play. The subchapter examines the interests of individual NATO member states, regional powers, and international organizations involved in the military intervention.

One key aspect of the examination is the role of intelligence in shaping the political motivations behind Operation Odyssey Down. The subchapter analyzes how intelligence reports, assessments, and analysis influenced the decision-making processes and provided the justification for military intervention. It also explores the potential biases and limitations of intelligence in understanding the complex political dynamics on the ground.

Furthermore, this subchapter critically evaluates the humanitarian aspects of the military intervention in Libya. It examines the extent to which the protection of civilian lives and the prevention of mass atrocities were genuinely prioritized over other political and strategic objectives. It also investigates the effectiveness of the international coalition in achieving its stated humanitarian goals.

The subchapter also explores the impact of Operation Odyssey Down on regional stability in North Africa. It assesses the unintended consequences of the military intervention, such as the proliferation of weapons and the spillover of violence into neighboring countries. By examining these regional dynamics, historians can gain a deeper understanding of the long-term implications of the military operation.

Additionally, the subchapter analyzes the legal and ethical implications of the intervention. It examines the extent to which the military operation complied with international law and ethical standards, as well as the controversies surrounding the intervention's legality.

Ultimately, this subchapter provides historians with a comprehensive and nuanced examination of the political motivations behind Operation Odyssey Down. By uncovering the complex political dynamics that shaped this military operation, historians can gain valuable insights into the decision-making processes and objectives of the international coalition during this pivotal moment in history.

Examination of Political Motivations in Unified Protector

The subchapter titled "Examination of Political Motivations in Unified Protector" delves into the intricate web of political motivations that drove the NATO-led military operation in Libya in 2011. Addressing an audience of historians and focusing on the broader context of Operation Unified Protector, this chapter seeks to unravel the underlying political dynamics that shaped and influenced the intervention.

In order to understand the political motivations behind Unified Protector, it is vital to analyze the historical background and events leading up to the military operation. The chapter will explore the factors that prompted NATO to intervene in Libya, including the Arab Spring uprisings, the Libyan civil war, and the subsequent threat to regional stability in North Africa. By examining the strategic goals and outcomes of Unified Protector, a comprehensive assessment of the political motivations can be established.

Drawing upon a range of primary and secondary sources, the chapter will provide an in-depth analysis of the political considerations that influenced the decision-making process within NATO member states. It will explore the role of key international actors, such as the United States, France, and the United Kingdom, in shaping the political motivations behind the military intervention. Additionally, the chapter will evaluate the effectiveness of the international coalition in achieving its objectives in Libya, shedding light on the complexities of multilateral military operations.

Furthermore, the subchapter will critically assess the legal and ethical implications of the interventions in Libya, examining the justifications put forth by the international community and the extent to which these aligned with the principles of the Responsibility to Protect. By examining the humanitarian aspects of the interventions, the chapter will evaluate the impact of the military operations on the civilian population and the extent to which their security and well-being were safeguarded.

Finally, the subchapter will explore the post-conflict reconstruction efforts in Libya following the NATO-led military interventions. It will examine the role of the United Nations in supporting and coordinating these efforts, and evaluate the successes and failures in rebuilding the nation. This analysis will shed light on the long-term consequences of the political motivations behind Unified Protector and their impact on the stability and future of Libya.

Overall, the subchapter "Examination of Political Motivations in Unified Protector" offers a comprehensive exploration of the complex political dynamics that shaped the NATO-led military operation in Libya. By analyzing the motivations behind the intervention, its legal and ethical implications, and the post-conflict reconstruction efforts, this chapter provides historians with valuable insights into the multifaceted nature of Operation Unified Protector.

Chapter 4: Evaluation of the Humanitarian Aspects of the Interventions in Libya

Humanitarian Crisis in Libya

The humanitarian crisis in Libya was a central aspect of the two NATO-led military operations, Operations Odyssey Down and Unified Protector, that took place in 2011. This subchapter aims to delve into the various dimensions of this crisis and shed light on its impact on the Libyan population, regional stability in North Africa, and the effectiveness of the international coalition's objectives.

The crisis in Libya was characterized by widespread violence, displacement, and a severe threat to civilian lives. The book explores the role of intelligence in understanding the nature and scale of the crisis, as well as its implications for the strategic goals and outcomes of the military operations. It also provides an analysis of the political motivations behind NATO's decision to intervene in Libya, considering the legal and ethical implications of such interventions.

Furthermore, the subchapter evaluates the humanitarian aspects of the interventions, assessing the effectiveness of the international coalition in protecting civilian lives and providing aid to those affected by the crisis. It also examines the role of the United Nations in supporting and coordinating the military operations, highlighting its efforts in facilitating post-conflict reconstruction in Libya.

The impact of the military operations on regional stability in North Africa is another crucial aspect explored in this subchapter. It analyzes the consequences of the interventions on neighboring countries, such as the influx of refugees, the proliferation of weapons, and the rise of extremist groups. By studying the role of air power in both operations, the book uncovers the strategic and tactical considerations that influenced the use of this military tool.

Finally, the subchapter compares the strategic goals and outcomes of Operations Odyssey Down and Unified Protector, highlighting the similarities and differences between the two military operations. It critically evaluates the effectiveness of the international coalition in achieving its objectives and identifies lessons learned for future interventions.

This subchapter offers historians and experts in the niches of Operations Odyssey Down and Unified Protector a comprehensive analysis of the humanitarian crisis in Libya and its implications. It contributes to a deeper understanding of the complex dynamics at play during these military interventions, shedding light on the challenges faced and the lessons to be learned for future interventions and post-conflict reconstruction efforts.

NATO's Humanitarian Mandate

One of the key aspects of the NATO-led military operations in Libya was its humanitarian mandate. The international community, led by NATO, intervened in Libya in 2011 to protect civilians from the violence perpetrated by the regime of Muammar Gaddafi. This subchapter aims to analyze and evaluate the humanitarian aspects of these interventions.

The humanitarian mandate of NATO's operations in Libya was rooted in the principles of the Responsibility to Protect (R2P), which states that the international community has a responsibility to protect populations from mass atrocities. In the case of Libya, the Gaddafi regime's brutal crackdown on peaceful protesters and the potential for widespread violence necessitated a swift response to protect civilians.

NATO's military intervention aimed to enforce a no-fly zone and implement an arms embargo to prevent the Gaddafi regime from using its air power and heavy weaponry against civilians. Additionally, NATO forces provided critical support to opposition forces, enabling them to counter Gaddafi's forces and eventually overthrow his regime.

The effectiveness of NATO's humanitarian mandate in Libya is a subject of debate among historians. While the intervention successfully prevented a potential massacre in the city of Benghazi, critics argue that the mission expanded beyond its original scope, leading to unintended consequences and a prolonged conflict.

Furthermore, the humanitarian aspects of the NATO-led interventions must be evaluated in the context of the post-conflict reconstruction efforts in Libya. Following Gaddafi's fall, the country descended into chaos, with rival factions vying for power and extremist groups exploiting the power vacuum. This raises questions about the long-term impact of the military operations on regional stability in North Africa.

Moreover, the legal and ethical implications of the interventions in Libya must be examined. Critics argue that NATO exceeded its UN Security Council mandate by actively supporting opposition forces and participating in regime change. The intervention also raised concerns about the potential for future abuses of the R2P principle.

In conclusion, the humanitarian mandate of NATO's operations in Libya was driven by the need to protect civilians from mass atrocities. However, the effectiveness and consequences of this intervention remain subjects of debate. Evaluating the humanitarian aspects of the interventions in Libya requires an examination of their impact on regional stability, the legal and ethical implications, and the post-conflict reconstruction efforts in the country.

Assessment of Humanitarian Efforts in Operations Odyssey Down

Humanitarian efforts play a crucial role in military operations, particularly when it comes to mitigating the impact of conflict on civilian populations. In the case of Operations Odyssey Down, the NATO-led military intervention in Libya in 2011, assessing the effectiveness of humanitarian efforts is of paramount importance. This subchapter aims to evaluate the humanitarian aspects of the interventions in Libya, focusing specifically on Operation Odyssey Down.

The humanitarian situation in Libya prior to the intervention was dire. Muammar Gaddafi's regime had unleashed a brutal crackdown on anti-government protests, resulting in widespread violence and displacement. In response, the international coalition launched military operations to protect civilians and enforce a no-fly zone. However, the assessment of the humanitarian efforts in Operation Odyssey Down reveals both successes and challenges.

One of the key successes of the humanitarian efforts in Operation Odyssey Down was the protection of civilian lives. The NATO-led coalition effectively targeted Gaddafi's military infrastructure, reducing the regime's ability to harm civilians. Furthermore, the enforcement of a no-fly zone prevented Gaddafi's forces from using aircraft to attack populated areas. These actions undoubtedly saved countless lives and contributed to the overall success of the mission.

However, challenges also emerged in the execution of humanitarian efforts. Despite attempts to minimize civilian casualties, there were instances where airstrikes resulted in unintended harm to non-combatants. This highlights the complex nature of military operations and the difficulty of ensuring the complete protection of civilians in a fluid and volatile conflict environment.

Additionally, the humanitarian situation in Libya deteriorated further after Gaddafi's regime was toppled. The absence of a comprehensive post-conflict stabilization plan created a power vacuum that led to further violence and instability. This highlights the importance of not only assessing the immediate impact of humanitarian efforts but also considering their long-term implications.

In conclusion, the assessment of humanitarian efforts in Operation Odyssey Down reveals a mixed picture. While the intervention successfully protected civilian lives and mitigated immediate harm, challenges persisted, particularly in minimizing unintended harm and addressing the long-term consequences of the conflict. Understanding these nuances is crucial for historians examining the role of humanitarian efforts in military operations and for policymakers seeking to improve future interventions.

Assessment of Humanitarian Efforts in Unified Protector

The subchapter titled "Assessment of Humanitarian Efforts in Unified Protector" delves into the evaluation of the humanitarian aspects of the NATO-led military intervention in Libya in 2011. This chapter aims to provide a comprehensive analysis of the effectiveness of these efforts, as well as their impact on the civilian population and the overall humanitarian situation in the country.

The humanitarian dimension of Unified Protector was a crucial aspect of the NATO-led military operations in Libya. As historians, it is essential to critically examine the strategies and actions taken by the international coalition to protect civilians and alleviate human suffering during the conflict.

This subchapter will assess the humanitarian efforts in Unified Protector by analyzing the coordination of humanitarian aid, the protection of vulnerable groups, and the provision of essential services such as healthcare, food, and shelter. It will also explore the challenges faced by humanitarian organizations and the military in delivering assistance in a complex and volatile environment.

Furthermore, this chapter will evaluate the impact of the military operations on the civilian population, including the number of casualties, displacement, and access to basic necessities. It will also consider the long-term consequences of the intervention on the humanitarian situation in Libya, such as the disruption of essential infrastructure and the exacerbation of existing socio-economic challenges.

To provide a comprehensive assessment, this subchapter will draw upon various sources, including official reports, academic studies, and testimonies from humanitarian actors on the ground. The analysis will also consider the perspectives of local communities and the Libyan government regarding the humanitarian efforts and their effectiveness.

By critically evaluating the humanitarian aspects of Unified Protector, this subchapter aims to contribute to a nuanced understanding of the impact of the NATO-led military intervention in Libya. It will shed light on the successes and shortcomings of the humanitarian efforts, providing valuable insights for future interventions and humanitarian operations in similar contexts.

Overall, this subchapter will serve as a valuable resource for historians interested in understanding the complexities of humanitarian interventions and their implications for conflict-affected populations.

Chapter 5: Impact of the Military Operations on Regional Stability in North Africa

Pre-existing Regional Dynamics in North Africa

The subchapter on "Pre-existing Regional Dynamics in North Africa" in the book "From Odyssey to Protector: Unraveling the Two NATO-led Military Operations in Libya" provides a comprehensive analysis of the historical and geopolitical context of North Africa before the two NATO-led military operations in Libya in 2011. This chapter is primarily targeted at historians and readers interested in understanding the complex dynamics that shaped the region and influenced the outcomes of the interventions.

The chapter begins by delving into the historical background of North Africa, highlighting the centuries-long influence of colonial powers, the struggle for independence, and the subsequent emergence of various political systems in the region. It explores the impact of these historical events on the region's political and social fabric, setting the stage for the subsequent analysis of the NATO-led military interventions.

The subchapter then examines the regional dynamics that existed prior to the interventions, focusing on the relationships between North African countries and their neighboring states. It explores the historical rivalries, alliances, and conflicts that played a significant role in shaping the regional balance of power. The chapter also analyzes the role of non-state actors, such as armed groups and transnational terrorist organizations operating in the region, highlighting their influence on regional stability.

Furthermore, the subchapter discusses the economic dynamics of the region, including the significance of oil and gas reserves in North Africa and their impact on regional politics and international relations. It explores the interdependence of North African countries in terms of energy resources, trade, and economic cooperation, and how these factors influenced the regional dynamics prior to the interventions.

The chapter concludes by drawing connections between the pre-existing regional dynamics and the objectives and outcomes of the NATO-led military operations in Libya. It highlights how the regional context influenced the decision-making process of NATO member states and their motivations for intervening in Libya.

Overall, the subchapter on "Pre-existing Regional Dynamics in North Africa" provides historians and readers interested in the NATO-led military operations in Libya with a comprehensive understanding of the historical, geopolitical, and economic factors that shaped the region before the interventions. By analyzing these dynamics, the chapter lays the foundation for a deeper understanding of the subsequent chapters that explore the various aspects and implications of the military operations and their impact on the region.

Consequences of the NATO-led Interventions

The NATO-led military interventions in Libya, known as Operations Odyssey Down and Unified Protector, have had far-reaching consequences across various aspects. From the political motivations behind these operations to the impact on regional stability in North Africa, the consequences of these interventions have been both profound and controversial.

One of the key consequences of these interventions was the role of intelligence in shaping the operations. Historians have analyzed the intelligence gathering and analysis process during Operations Odyssey Down and Unified Protector, shedding light on the successes and failures in the utilization of intelligence resources. This subchapter delves

into the significance of intelligence in guiding the NATO-led
interventions and its impact on the overall outcomes.

Moreover, the political motivations behind these operations have been
subject to scrutiny. Historians have analyzed the complex web of
alliances and interests that led to the decision to intervene in Libya.
Through a detailed analysis, this subchapter provides a comprehensive
understanding of the political dynamics at play during the NATO-led
interventions.

Another crucial aspect examined in this subchapter is the evaluation of
the humanitarian aspects of these interventions. Historians delve into
the ethical implications of the military operations and assess the
effectiveness of the international coalition in achieving its humanitarian
objectives. The subchapter also examines the role of the United Nations
in supporting and coordinating these military operations, shedding light
on the challenges and successes faced during the implementation.

The impact of the military operations on regional stability in North
Africa is also a vital area of analysis. Historians assess the repercussions
of these interventions on neighboring countries, examining the potential
for geopolitical shifts and power struggles. The examination of the
post-conflict reconstruction efforts in Libya following the NATO-led
interventions is also addressed, highlighting the challenges faced during
the rebuilding process.

Furthermore, this subchapter compares the strategic goals and outcomes
of the two NATO-led military operations in Libya. By analyzing the
similarities and differences between Operations Odyssey Down and
Unified Protector, historians gain insights into the effectiveness of
different strategies employed.

Finally, the subchapter delves into the legal and ethical implications of
the interventions in Libya. Historians examine the adherence to

international law and ethical standards during the operations, assessing the controversies and potential ramifications.

In conclusion, this subchapter on the consequences of the NATO-led interventions in Libya provides a comprehensive analysis for historians and individuals interested in understanding the multifaceted outcomes of Operations Odyssey Down and Unified Protector. From political motivations to humanitarian aspects and regional stability, this subchapter offers unique insights into the complexities of these military interventions.

Analysis of Regional Stability in the Aftermath of Operations Odyssey Down

The subchapter titled "Analysis of Regional Stability in the Aftermath of Operations Odyssey Down" delves into the impact of the NATO-led military operations in Libya on regional stability in North Africa. This analysis is of particular interest to historians and those interested in the broader context of the Operations Odyssey Down and Unified Protector.

The military interventions in Libya, especially Operation Odyssey Down, aimed to protect civilians from the oppressive regime of Muammar Gaddafi. However, the consequences of these operations went beyond their immediate objectives. The subchapter explores the regional stability implications of these military interventions.

One of the key aspects examined in this analysis is the role of intelligence in the decision-making process leading up to the military operations. Understanding how intelligence was utilized and the accuracy of the information available provides crucial insights into the motivations behind the interventions.

Furthermore, the subchapter delves into the political motivations that drove NATO's involvement in Libya. It evaluates the various factors that influenced the decision to intervene and assesses the implications for regional stability.

Additionally, the humanitarian aspects of the interventions are evaluated. The subchapter examines the effectiveness of the international coalition in achieving its objectives and analyzes the legal and ethical implications of the military operations. This analysis sheds light on the complexities and challenges faced by the international community when intervening in a conflict to protect civilian lives.

The subchapter also considers the role of air power in both Operations Odyssey Down and Unified Protector. By examining the strategic goals and outcomes of these operations, it provides a comparison between the two interventions and their impact on regional stability.

Moreover, the study delves into the role of the United Nations in supporting and coordinating the military operations in Libya. It evaluates the effectiveness of the UN in facilitating a coordinated international response and the implications for regional stability.

Lastly, the subchapter examines the post-conflict reconstruction efforts in Libya following the military interventions. It evaluates the effectiveness of these efforts and their impact on regional stability in North Africa.

Overall, the analysis of regional stability in the aftermath of Operations Odyssey Down provides crucial insights into the broader consequences of the NATO-led military operations in Libya. By examining various aspects such as intelligence, political motivations, humanitarian aspects, air power, legal and ethical implications, the role of the United Nations, and post-conflict reconstruction efforts, historians and those interested in the Operations Odyssey Down and Unified Protector gain a comprehensive understanding of the impact of these interventions on regional stability in North Africa.

Analysis of Regional Stability in the Aftermath of Unified Protector

The NATO-led military operations in Libya, known as Operations Odyssey Down and Unified Protector, had a significant impact on regional stability in North Africa. In the aftermath of Unified Protector, it is crucial to analyze the effects of these military interventions on the region.

The primary objective of Unified Protector was to protect Libyan civilians from the violence perpetrated by the Gaddafi regime. However, the intervention had unintended consequences, which affected regional stability. The power vacuum created after the fall of Gaddafi led to the emergence of various armed groups, militias, and extremist organizations. These groups capitalized on the chaos and instability, further exacerbating the security situation in Libya and its neighboring countries.

The proliferation of weapons and the flow of fighters across borders has posed a severe threat to regional stability. Libya has become a breeding ground for extremist ideologies, and terrorist organizations, such as ISIS, have found safe havens in the country. The instability in Libya has also had a spill-over effect on neighboring countries, leading to increased violence and instability in the region.

The political motivations behind the NATO-led military operations in Libya must also be examined to understand their impact on regional stability. While the protection of civilians was the stated goal, there were underlying geopolitical interests at play. Some argue that the interventions were driven by a desire to secure access to Libya's oil reserves or to prevent the spread of instability to Europe. These political motivations can have long-lasting implications for regional stability.

Furthermore, the effectiveness of the international coalition in achieving its objectives in Libya needs to be evaluated. The military operations were successful in overthrowing the Gaddafi regime, but they failed to establish a stable and secure environment in the country. The lack of a comprehensive post-conflict reconstruction plan and the failure to address the underlying political and social issues in Libya contributed to the ongoing instability.

In conclusion, the military operations in Libya, specifically Operations Odyssey Down and Unified Protector, have had a significant impact on regional stability in North Africa. The power vacuum and the proliferation of armed groups have created a breeding ground for extremism and terrorism. The political motivations behind the interventions and the effectiveness of the international coalition must be scrutinized to understand the implications for regional stability. Additionally, the examination of post-conflict reconstruction efforts in Libya is essential to address the underlying issues and restore stability in the region.

Chapter 6: Examination of the Role of Air Power in Operations Odyssey Down and Unified Protector

Significance of Air Power in Modern Warfare

Chapter Title: Significance of Air Power in Modern Warfare

Introduction:

The use of air power has emerged as a crucial aspect of modern warfare, shaping the outcomes of military operations and influencing regional stability. This subchapter explores the significance of air power in the context of the two 2011 NATO-led military operations in Libya, namely Operations Odyssey Down and Unified Protector. By analyzing the strategic goals, outcomes, and impact of these interventions, this subchapter sheds light on the role of air power in contemporary conflicts.

Understanding Air Power:

Air power encompasses a range of military capabilities, including aerial surveillance, intelligence gathering, strategic bombing, close air support, and air superiority. With its ability to rapidly project force over great distances, air power has become an integral component of modern military operations.

Strategic Goals and Outcomes:

The subchapter delves into a comparative analysis of the strategic goals and outcomes of Operations Odyssey Down and Unified Protector. By examining the role of air power in achieving these objectives, it becomes evident that air power played a pivotal role in both operations, facilitating the enforcement of no-fly zones, neutralizing enemy air defenses, and providing support to ground forces.

Impact on Regional Stability:

The use of air power in Libya had far-reaching implications for regional stability in North Africa. The subchapter explores the impact of these military operations on neighboring countries, such as Egypt, Tunisia, and Algeria, as well as the broader implications for the region's security dynamics.

Ethical and Legal Implications:

Examining the legal and ethical dimensions of the interventions in Libya, this subchapter scrutinizes the adherence to international humanitarian law and the responsibility to protect civilians. It evaluates the effectiveness of the international coalition in minimizing civilian casualties and avoiding collateral damage.

The Role of Air Power in Humanitarian Interventions:

Air power also played a crucial role in facilitating humanitarian aspects during the interventions. This subchapter evaluates the effectiveness of air power in delivering humanitarian aid, evacuating civilians, and protecting vulnerable populations.

Role of the United Nations and Post-Conflict Reconstruction:

The subchapter discusses the role of the United Nations in supporting and coordinating the military operations in Libya. Furthermore, it examines the post-conflict reconstruction efforts in Libya following the NATO-led military interventions, with a particular focus on the challenges and successes in rebuilding the country's infrastructure and institutions.

Conclusion:

In conclusion, the significance of air power in modern warfare cannot be overstated. This subchapter highlights its pivotal role in Operations Odyssey Down and Unified Protector, emphasizing its impact on achieving strategic goals, maintaining regional stability, and addressing humanitarian concerns. By delving into the legal, ethical, and practical implications of air power, this subchapter provides a comprehensive analysis for historians and scholars interested in understanding the multifaceted nature of modern military operations.

Air Operations in Operations Odyssey Down

The subchapter "Air Operations in Operations Odyssey Down" delves into the significant role of air power in the NATO-led military intervention in Libya in 2011. This section aims to provide a comprehensive analysis of the air operations conducted during Operations Odyssey Down, highlighting their strategic importance, outcomes, and impact on the overall mission.

During the initial phase of Operations Odyssey Down, air operations played a crucial role in establishing air superiority over Libya. The NATO coalition deployed a wide range of aircraft, including fighter jets, bombers, and unmanned aerial vehicles, to enforce a no-fly zone and protect civilian populations from the brutal attacks of Muammar Gaddafi's regime. The use of air power was an essential component in neutralizing Gaddafi's air defenses, destroying his military infrastructure, and disrupting his command and control capabilities.

The subchapter will explore the coordination and integration of air assets from various NATO member states, emphasizing the importance of joint operations and the pooling of resources. It will also discuss the challenges faced by NATO air forces, such as the need to minimize civilian casualties and collateral damage while conducting precision airstrikes.

Furthermore, this section will examine the impact of air operations on the overall outcomes of Operations Odyssey Down. It will analyze how the successful implementation of the no-fly zone and the destruction of key military targets contributed to the eventual downfall of the Gaddafi regime. The subchapter will also evaluate the effectiveness of air power in reducing civilian casualties and protecting vulnerable populations.

Additionally, the subchapter will compare and contrast the strategic goals and outcomes of Operations Odyssey Down with the subsequent NATO-led military operation in Libya, Unified Protector. By examining the similarities and differences between these two operations, historians can gain a deeper understanding of the evolution of NATO's intervention in Libya and its implications for future military interventions.

In conclusion, the subchapter "Air Operations in Operations Odyssey Down" sheds light on the critical role of air power in the NATO-led military intervention in Libya. It provides historians with valuable insights into the strategic importance of air operations, their impact on the overall mission, and their contribution to achieving the objectives of the international coalition.

Air Operations in Unified Protector

The subchapter on "Air Operations in Unified Protector" delves into the crucial role played by air power in the NATO-led military intervention in Libya in 2011. This section examines the strategic goals, outcomes, and effectiveness of the air operations, while also analyzing the legal and ethical implications of such interventions.

Unified Protector marked the second NATO-led military operation in Libya, following the earlier Operation Odyssey Dawn. It aimed to protect civilians, enforce an arms embargo, and establish a no-fly zone to prevent the regime of Muammar Gaddafi from attacking his own people. Air power became the primary tool to achieve these objectives.

The air operations in Unified Protector were characterized by a range of assets, including fighter jets, attack helicopters, unmanned aerial vehicles (UAVs), and aerial refueling capabilities. These assets were deployed from various NATO member countries and coordinated under a unified command structure.

The subchapter explores the impact of air power on the conflict, analyzing its effectiveness in neutralizing Gaddafi's military capabilities and protecting civilians. It delves into the strategic goals of the air operations, such as disrupting command and control structures, destroying air defense systems, and targeting key military installations. It also evaluates the outcomes of these goals and their contribution to the overall success of the intervention.

Furthermore, the subchapter examines the legal and ethical implications of the air operations. It delves into the debates surrounding the justification for military intervention, the adherence to international law, and the protection of civilian lives. It analyzes the proportionality of the use of force and the efforts made to minimize collateral damage.

In addition, the subchapter assesses the impact of the air operations on regional stability in North Africa. It examines the unintended consequences of the intervention, such as the proliferation of arms and the rise of non-state actors. It also explores the challenges faced in transitioning from military operations to post-conflict reconstruction efforts.

Overall, this subchapter provides a comprehensive analysis of the role of air power in Unified Protector, shedding light on its strategic goals, outcomes, legal implications, and impact on regional stability. It offers valuable insights for historians and researchers interested in understanding the complexities of NATO-led military interventions and their consequences.

Chapter 7: Comparison of the Strategic Goals and Outcomes of the Two NATO-led Military Operations in Libya

Strategic Objectives of Operations Odyssey Down

Introduction:

The subchapter titled "Strategic Objectives of Operations Odyssey Down" aims to provide a comprehensive analysis of the goals and objectives behind the NATO-led military operation in Libya, referred to as Operations Odyssey Down. This subchapter will delve into the strategic objectives set forth by the international coalition and examine their significance and impact on the overall outcome of the mission.

Content:

1. Contextualizing Operations Odyssey Down:

- Brief overview of the political and humanitarian crisis in Libya that led to the military intervention.

- Explanation of the need for international coalition involvement.

2. Defining Strategic Objectives:

- Identification and analysis of the key strategic objectives of Operations Odyssey Down.

- Highlighting the importance of these objectives in achieving the desired outcomes.

3. Military Objectives:

- Examination of the military goals set by the international coalition.

- Evaluation of the role of air power in achieving these objectives.

- Analysis of the impact of these objectives on regional stability in North Africa.

4. Humanitarian Objectives:

- Discussion of the humanitarian aspects of the intervention.

- Evaluation of the effectiveness of the international coalition in addressing the humanitarian crisis.

- Examination of the ethical implications of the military operations and their impact on civilian populations.

5. Political Objectives:

- Analysis of the political motivations behind NATO-led military operations in Libya.

- Assessment of the role of the United Nations in supporting and coordinating the military operations.

- Evaluation of the effectiveness of the international coalition in achieving its political goals.

6. Comparative Analysis with Unified Protector:

- Comparison of the strategic goals and outcomes of Operations Odyssey Down with its successor, Unified Protector.

- Examination of the similarities and differences in strategic objectives between the two operations.

7. Legal and Ethical Implications:

- Analysis of the legal and ethical considerations surrounding the military interventions in Libya.

- Evaluation of the adherence to international law and ethical standards during the operations.

8. Post-Conflict Reconstruction Efforts:

- Study of the post-conflict reconstruction efforts in Libya following the NATO-led military interventions.

- Assessment of the effectiveness and challenges faced in rebuilding Libya.

Conclusion:

This subchapter provides a comprehensive exploration of the strategic objectives of Operations Odyssey Down, shedding light on the military, humanitarian, and political goals set by the international coalition. By evaluating the impact and effectiveness of these objectives, historians and readers interested in the niche of Operations Odyssey Down will gain a deeper understanding of the complexities and outcomes of this NATO-led military operation in Libya.

Strategic Objectives of Unified Protector

The subchapter titled "Strategic Objectives of Unified Protector" aims to provide a comprehensive analysis of the goals and outcomes of the NATO-led military operation in Libya known as Unified Protector. This section of the book "From Odyssey to Protector: Unraveling the Two NATO-led Military Operations in Libya" is targeted towards historians and individuals interested in understanding the intricacies of military operations in Libya, with a specific focus on Unified Protector.

The subchapter begins by delving into the strategic objectives that NATO aimed to achieve through Unified Protector. It explores the primary goal of protecting civilian lives and populations in Libya, as mandated by United Nations Security Council Resolution 1973. The content delves into the importance of this objective in the context of the ongoing conflict in Libya and the need for international intervention to prevent further humanitarian crises.

Furthermore, the subchapter analyzes the secondary strategic objectives of Unified Protector, such as the enforcement of an arms embargo, the establishment of a no-fly zone, and the protection of critical infrastructure. It examines the rationale behind these objectives and their impact on the overall mission.

The content also explores the outcomes of Unified Protector, evaluating the extent to which these strategic objectives were achieved. It assesses the effectiveness of the international coalition in achieving its goals and the role of air power in contributing to the success of the operation. Additionally, it examines the legal and ethical implications of the intervention, shedding light on the debates surrounding the use of military force for humanitarian purposes.

To provide a comprehensive understanding of the subject matter, the subchapter compares the strategic goals and outcomes of Unified Protector with those of Operation Odyssey Dawn, the initial NATO-led military operation in Libya. It highlights the similarities and differences between the two operations, offering insights into the evolving nature of the conflict and the international response.

Finally, the subchapter concludes by examining the impact of Unified Protector on regional stability in North Africa. It evaluates the long-term consequences of the military operation and its role in shaping the political landscape of the region. Additionally, it explores the post-conflict reconstruction efforts in Libya, analyzing the challenges and successes of the international community in supporting Libya's transition to stability and peace.

Overall, this subchapter provides historians and individuals interested in military operations and international interventions in Libya with a comprehensive analysis of the strategic objectives and outcomes of Unified Protector. It offers valuable insights into the complexities of the operation and its impact on the region as a whole.

Comparison of Outcomes and Achievements

In this subchapter, we will delve into the comparison of outcomes and achievements between two NATO-led military operations in Libya: Operations Odyssey Down and Unified Protector. As historians, it is crucial to assess the impact and effectiveness of these interventions, considering their historical significance and relevance.

Both operations were carried out in 2011, with the primary objective of protecting civilians and supporting the Libyan people in their struggle for freedom and democracy. However, there were notable differences in the execution and strategic goals of these operations.

Operation Odyssey Down primarily focused on the evacuation and extraction of foreign nationals from Libya, ensuring their safety during the escalating conflict. This mission was successfully accomplished, with thousands of individuals being safely repatriated to their home countries. The operation showcased the swift response and coordination of the international coalition, highlighting the importance of intelligence in executing such operations.

In contrast, Operation Unified Protector aimed to enforce a no-fly zone and protect civilians from the Gaddafi regime's aggression. This operation involved a sustained air campaign and close coordination between NATO forces and rebel groups on the ground. The strategic goal was to weaken Gaddafi's military capabilities and ultimately facilitate the regime's overthrow. The intervention successfully weakened

Gaddafi's forces and provided crucial support to the rebel groups, leading to the eventual collapse of the regime.

The humanitarian aspects of these interventions were crucial in the assessment of their outcomes. While both operations aimed to protect civilians, there were instances of collateral damage and civilian casualties. The evaluation of these aspects requires a nuanced understanding of the complexities and challenges faced by the international coalition.

Moreover, the impact of these military operations on regional stability in North Africa cannot be overlooked. The interventions in Libya had far-reaching consequences, leading to a power vacuum and subsequent destabilization in the region. This raises important questions about the long-term implications and the need for post-conflict reconstruction efforts.

By comparing the strategic goals, outcomes, and achievements of Operations Odyssey Down and Unified Protector, we can gain valuable insights into the effectiveness of the international coalition in achieving its objectives. Additionally, analyzing the legal and ethical implications of these interventions is crucial to understanding the role of the United Nations in supporting and coordinating military operations in Libya.

In conclusion, this subchapter provides a comprehensive analysis of the outcomes and achievements of two NATO-led military operations in Libya. By examining various factors such as intelligence, political motivations, humanitarian aspects, regional stability, air power, legal and ethical implications, effectiveness of the international coalition, and post-conflict reconstruction efforts, historians can gain a deeper understanding of these interventions and their historical significance.

Chapter 8: Analysis of the Legal and Ethical Implications of the Interventions in Libya

International Law and Justifications for Intervention

In the realm of international relations and conflicts, the role of international law and the justifications for intervention are crucial aspects that shape the decisions and actions of nations and organizations. The NATO-led military operations in Libya in 2011, namely Operations Odyssey Down and Unified Protector, provide a rich case study to explore these dimensions. This subchapter delves into the legal and ethical implications of these interventions, examining the justifications put forth by the international coalition and their adherence to international law.

At the heart of any military intervention lies the question of legality. Under the United Nations Charter, the use of force is only permitted in cases of self-defense or when authorized by the UN Security Council. The NATO-led operations in Libya were carried out under the legal umbrella of two UN Security Council resolutions, 1970 and 1973, which aimed to protect civilians and enforce a no-fly zone. These resolutions were based on the principle of the Responsibility to Protect (R2P), which asserts that states have a duty to protect their populations from mass atrocities and that the international community has a responsibility to intervene when states fail to do so.

However, the legal justifications for intervention are not without controversy. Critics argue that the interpretation and implementation of these resolutions went beyond their original intent, leading to a mission creep that exceeded the scope of civilian protection. Additionally, concerns were raised about the lack of a clear exit strategy and the potential for unintended consequences, such as the destabilization of the region.

Ethically, the interventions in Libya were framed as necessary to prevent a humanitarian catastrophe. The regime of Muammar Gaddafi was accused of committing widespread human rights abuses and engaging in a brutal crackdown on dissent. By intervening, the international coalition sought to uphold the principles of human rights and protect the civilian population from further harm.

However, ethical considerations are not always straightforward. Critics argue that the interventions in Libya were driven by geopolitical interests rather than purely humanitarian concerns. The role of intelligence in shaping the decision-making process and the analysis of political motivations behind the operations are critical in understanding the complex dynamics at play.

In conclusion, the legal and ethical dimensions of the NATO-led military operations in Libya are vital areas of inquiry for historians and scholars. By examining the justifications for intervention through the lens of international law, the role of intelligence, and the analysis of political motivations, a comprehensive understanding of the decision-making process can be achieved. Furthermore, evaluating the effectiveness of the international coalition in achieving its objectives, the impact on regional stability, and the post-conflict reconstruction efforts allows for a comprehensive assessment of the long-term consequences of these interventions.

Examination of Legal and Ethical Concerns in Operations Odyssey Down

The NATO-led military operations in Libya, known as Operations Odyssey Down, have been subject to scrutiny and analysis by historians and various niche groups. One crucial aspect to consider is the examination of the legal and ethical concerns that arose during this operation.

From a legal perspective, the interventions in Libya raised questions about the extent of NATO's mandate and the legitimacy of its actions. The United Nations Security Council Resolution 1973 authorized the establishment of a no-fly zone to protect civilians, but the subsequent escalation of military actions went beyond the initial scope. Some argued that this was a violation of international law and sovereignty of the Libyan state. The lack of a clear legal framework for intervention in cases of civil unrest further complicated the legal landscape.

Ethically, the interventions in Libya also raised concerns about the protection of civilians and the potential for collateral damage. While the initial objective was to prevent the massacre of civilians, there were instances where civilian casualties occurred. This raised questions about the ethical implications of military actions, particularly when it came to the use of air power and precision strikes. Critics argued that the pursuit of military objectives should not come at the expense of civilian lives.

Furthermore, the interventions in Libya also had political motivations that must be examined. The strategic goals and outcomes of the operation need to be analyzed in order to understand the broader context. Some argue that the interventions were driven by geopolitical interests and the desire to protect Western economic and political influence in the region. This raises questions about the extent to which humanitarian concerns were genuinely prioritized.

Lastly, the impact of the military operations on regional stability in North Africa should not be overlooked. While the interventions aimed to bring stability and protect civilians, they also contributed to a power vacuum and the proliferation of armed militias. This had implications not only for Libya but also for neighboring countries, such as Mali, where the conflict spilled over.

In conclusion, the examination of legal and ethical concerns in Operations Odyssey Down is essential to fully understand the complexities and implications of the NATO-led military interventions in Libya. By evaluating the legal framework, ethical considerations, political motivations, and regional impact, historians and niche groups can shed light on the successes, failures, and lessons learned from these operations.

Examination of Legal and Ethical Concerns in Unified Protector

The NATO-led military operation in Libya, known as Unified Protector, was a pivotal event in modern history that raised significant legal and ethical concerns. This subchapter aims to delve into the complexities surrounding the legal and ethical implications of the intervention, providing historians and scholars with a comprehensive understanding of the challenges faced during this period.

The legal dimension of Unified Protector is a subject of immense importance. The operation was conducted under the framework of United Nations Security Council Resolution 1973, which authorized the establishment of a no-fly zone and the protection of civilians. However, questions were raised regarding the interpretation and implementation of the resolution. Critics argued that NATO's actions went beyond the initial scope, leading to concerns of a mission creep and potential violation of international law. The subchapter will thoroughly examine these arguments, analyzing the legal basis for the intervention and the extent to which it adhered to international norms.

Ethical considerations also played a significant role in Unified Protector. The primary objective of the operation was to protect Libyan civilians from the atrocities committed by the Gaddafi regime. However, the means employed to achieve this goal were not without controversy. The use of air power, although effective in minimizing civilian casualties, raised concerns about the proportionality and necessity of force.

Additionally, the subchapter will explore the ethical implications of the NATO-led coalition working with various rebel groups, some of which were accused of human rights violations themselves.

Furthermore, the subchapter will examine the challenges faced by the international coalition in effectively coordinating their efforts in Libya. The complexity of the conflict, the diverging interests of coalition members, and the lack of a unified command structure raised questions about the effectiveness of the intervention. It will evaluate the extent to which the coalition was successful in achieving its objectives and mitigating the humanitarian crisis.

Lastly, the subchapter will explore the post-conflict reconstruction efforts in Libya following the NATO-led military intervention. It will critically analyze the effectiveness of these efforts, addressing the legal and ethical challenges encountered during the stabilization and rebuilding phase.

Overall, the examination of legal and ethical concerns in Unified Protector provides an invaluable insight into the intricacies of this operation. By exploring the legal basis, ethical implications, and post-conflict challenges, historians can gain a comprehensive understanding of the complexities faced by the international community during this critical period in Libya's history.

Chapter 9: Evaluation of the Effectiveness of the International Coalition in Achieving its Objectives in Libya

Composition and Cooperation of the International Coalition

The international coalition that participated in the NATO-led military operations in Libya comprised a diverse range of countries with varying levels of involvement and contributions. This subchapter delves into the composition and cooperation of this coalition, analyzing the dynamics that shaped their collective efforts in achieving the objectives set forth in Libya.

The coalition consisted of nations from North America, Europe, and the Middle East, with the United States and several European countries taking center stage. These nations provided crucial military assets, including fighter jets, naval vessels, and intelligence capabilities, which were instrumental in the success of the operations. The cooperation between these countries was facilitated through NATO, which served as the coordinating body for the military interventions.

The diverse composition of the coalition presented both opportunities and challenges. On the one hand, the involvement of countries with different military capabilities and resources allowed for a broader range of operations, enabling the coalition to effectively enforce the no-fly zone and conduct airstrikes against key targets. On the other hand, the differing national interests and political motivations of the participating nations sometimes led to disagreements and delays in decision-making.

Despite these challenges, the international coalition demonstrated a remarkable level of cooperation throughout the operations. Regular meetings and consultations were held to coordinate military strategies, share intelligence, and address any emerging issues. This collaborative approach contributed to the overall effectiveness of the coalition in achieving its objectives.

Furthermore, the coalition benefited from the support and coordination provided by the United Nations. The UN Security Council resolutions passed in support of the military interventions provided a legal and political framework for the operations, while the UN's involvement in coordinating humanitarian efforts ensured a comprehensive approach to the crisis in Libya.

The success of the international coalition in achieving its objectives in Libya can be attributed, in large part, to the collective efforts and commitment of its member states. Despite their diverse interests and capabilities, these nations came together to address the humanitarian crisis and protect civilians in Libya. The collaboration between military forces, intelligence agencies, and international organizations demonstrated the potential for effective multilateral action in resolving conflicts and promoting stability.

This subchapter concludes by examining the lessons learned from the composition and cooperation of the international coalition in Libya. It highlights the importance of clear strategic goals, effective communication, and a shared understanding of the legal and ethical implications of military interventions. Moreover, it underscores the need for continued coordination and cooperation in post-conflict reconstruction efforts to ensure a sustainable and stable future for Libya.

Assessment of Coalition's Effectiveness in Operations Odyssey Down

In the subchapter "Assessment of Coalition's Effectiveness in Operations Odyssey Down," we will delve into the critical analysis of the international coalition's performance in achieving its objectives during the NATO-led military intervention in Libya in 2011. This assessment is of paramount importance for historians and those interested in understanding the intricacies of Operations Odyssey Down and its impact on the region.

The coalition's effectiveness in achieving its objectives is a multifaceted and complex issue. We will explore various dimensions, including military strategy, coordination among coalition members, and the role of air power in the operation. By examining these aspects, we can gain insights into the strengths and weaknesses of the coalition's approach.

One vital aspect to consider is the role of intelligence in Operations Odyssey Down. Intelligence played a significant role in shaping the coalition's decision-making process and operational planning. By analyzing the intelligence available to the coalition, we can evaluate the accuracy of the information and its impact on the effectiveness of the operation.

Furthermore, an analysis of the political motivations behind the NATO-led military operation in Libya is crucial. By examining the underlying reasons that led to the intervention, we can assess the strategic goals and outcomes of the operation. This evaluation will shed light on the extent to which the coalition achieved its objectives and the potential implications for future military interventions.

The humanitarian aspects of the interventions in Libya also warrant evaluation. Understanding the impact of the military operations on the civilian population is essential in assessing the overall effectiveness of the coalition. By examining the measures taken to protect civilians and provide humanitarian assistance, we can gauge the success of the coalition's efforts in this regard.

Additionally, we will explore the implications of the military operations on regional stability in North Africa. Assessing the consequences of the intervention on neighboring countries and the wider region will provide insights into the long-term impact of Operations Odyssey Down.

Lastly, the effectiveness of the international coalition in achieving its objectives will be critically evaluated. By examining the coordination among coalition members, the allocation of resources, and the overall success in achieving the stated goals, we can assess the coalition's effectiveness in realizing its mission.

This subchapter will contribute to the broader understanding of the NATO-led military intervention in Libya in 2011. Through a comprehensive assessment of the coalition's effectiveness, we aim to provide historians and specialists in this field with valuable insights into the complexities and outcomes of Operations Odyssey Down.

Assessment of Coalition's Effectiveness in Unified Protector

In the subchapter titled "Assessment of Coalition's Effectiveness in Unified Protector," we delve into the evaluation of the international coalition's performance in achieving its objectives during the NATO-led military operation in Libya. This analysis aims to provide historians and scholars interested in the intricacies of military interventions with a comprehensive understanding of the coalition's effectiveness.

The Unified Protector operation, conducted in 2011, was a response to the Libyan civil war and aimed to protect civilians, enforce a no-fly zone, and implement an arms embargo. To assess the coalition's effectiveness, multiple factors need to be considered, including the coordination and cooperation among coalition members, the military strategies employed, and the overall achievement of the operation's objectives.

One crucial aspect to evaluate is the coordination and cooperation among the coalition members. Historians will explore how well the participating nations collaborated, shared intelligence, and coordinated their military efforts. This analysis will shed light on the effectiveness of the coalition's command structure and its ability to achieve a unified approach towards the operation's goals.

Furthermore, the assessment will examine the military strategies employed during Unified Protector. This will involve an analysis of the utilization of air power, the effectiveness of naval operations, and the integration of ground forces. Historians will evaluate the coalition's ability to adapt to the evolving situation on the ground and the effectiveness of its tactical decisions in achieving the desired outcomes.

The subchapter will also explore the extent to which the coalition achieved its objectives in Libya. This assessment will consider the impact of the military intervention on regional stability in North Africa, the humanitarian aspects of the operation, and the post-conflict reconstruction efforts in Libya. By analyzing the outcomes against the initial objectives, historians can determine the overall effectiveness of the international coalition in accomplishing its mission.

Through a meticulous analysis of the coalition's effectiveness in Unified Protector, historians will gain valuable insights into the complexities of military interventions. This subchapter provides a comprehensive evaluation of the international coalition's performance, allowing scholars to understand the strengths, weaknesses, and lessons learned from this NATO-led military operation in Libya.

Chapter 10: Study of the Role of the United Nations in Supporting and Coordinating the Military Operations in Libya

UN's Involvement in the Libyan Crisis

The Libyan crisis of 2011 marked a turning point in the history of the United Nations' involvement in military operations. In this subchapter, we will delve into the role of the United Nations in supporting and coordinating the military interventions in Libya.

The UN's engagement in the Libyan crisis began with the passing of UN Security Council Resolution 1970 on February 26, 2011. This resolution imposed an arms embargo, travel bans, and asset freezes on key individuals associated with the regime of Muammar Gaddafi. It also referred the situation in Libya to the International Criminal Court (ICC), paving the way for potential war crimes investigations.

The subsequent UN Security Council Resolution 1973 on March 17, 2011, authorized the use of all necessary means to protect civilians and civilian-populated areas from Gaddafi's forces. This resolution provided the legal basis for the NATO-led military operations in Libya, known as Operations Odyssey Dawn and Unified Protector.

The UN's involvement in the military operations extended beyond the authorization of force. The United Nations Support Mission in Libya (UNSMIL) played a crucial role in coordinating humanitarian efforts and facilitating dialogue between conflicting parties. UNSMIL sought to assist the Libyan people in their transition towards democracy and stability, working closely with the Transitional National Council (TNC), the interim governing body established during the crisis.

The UN's engagement in Libya also involved post-conflict reconstruction efforts. The United Nations Development Programme (UNDP) and other UN agencies provided assistance in areas such as governance, rule of law, security sector reform, and economic recovery. These efforts aimed to rebuild Libyan institutions and support the country's transition towards a more inclusive and democratic system.

However, the UN's involvement in Libya was not without challenges. The military operations and subsequent post-conflict reconstruction efforts faced criticism for their effectiveness and the unintended consequences they brought about. Some argued that the interventions failed to achieve their objectives in the long term, as Libya descended into a protracted civil war and political instability.

In conclusion, the United Nations played a significant role in the Libyan crisis, both in terms of authorizing military force and coordinating post-conflict efforts. This subchapter will provide a comprehensive analysis of the UN's involvement, examining its successes, challenges, and the implications for future military interventions and peacebuilding efforts.

UN's Role in Facilitating Operations Odyssey Down

The UN's Role in Facilitating Operations Odyssey Down

The United Nations (UN) played a significant role in facilitating the NATO-led military operation known as Odyssey Down in Libya in 2011. This subchapter aims to analyze and evaluate the UN's involvement in this operation, addressing the interests of historians and those interested in the specific niche of Operation Odyssey Down.

The UN's role in facilitating military operations in Libya can be traced back to the initial stages of the conflict. As tensions escalated in Libya, the UN Security Council passed Resolution 1970, imposing an arms embargo and targeted sanctions on the Libyan government. This resolution also referred the situation in Libya to the International Criminal Court (ICC), highlighting the UN's commitment to accountability and justice.

Subsequently, the UN Security Council passed Resolution 1973, which authorized the implementation of a no-fly zone and the protection of civilians in Libya. This resolution formed the legal basis for NATO's military intervention, including Operation Odyssey Down. The UN's involvement in drafting and passing these resolutions demonstrated its commitment to addressing the humanitarian aspects of the conflict and ensuring the protection of Libyan civilians.

Furthermore, the UN played a crucial role in coordinating the international coalition involved in the military operations in Libya. The UN Secretary-General appointed a Special Envoy to Libya, whose responsibility was to facilitate communication and coordination between NATO and other international actors. This coordination was essential for the success of Operation Odyssey Down and the achievement of its objectives.

Moreover, the UN's involvement extended beyond the military intervention itself. The organization played a vital role in post-conflict reconstruction efforts in Libya. The UN provided humanitarian aid, facilitated political dialogue, and supported the establishment of a transitional government. This comprehensive approach aimed to stabilize the country and pave the way for a peaceful and democratic future.

In conclusion, the UN's role in facilitating Operation Odyssey Down in Libya was crucial in several aspects. From providing the legal framework for the military intervention to coordinating the international coalition and supporting post-conflict reconstruction, the UN played a pivotal role in ensuring the success of this operation. Historians and those interested in Operation Odyssey Down will find value in examining the

UN's multifaceted involvement and its impact on the outcome of the military operations and the subsequent reconstruction efforts in Libya.

UN's Role in Facilitating Unified Protector

The UN's Role in Facilitating Unified Protector

The United Nations (UN) played a crucial role in supporting and coordinating the military operations in Libya during the NATO-led mission known as Unified Protector. This subchapter aims to analyze the significance of the UN's involvement in the operation, particularly in terms of facilitating international cooperation, ensuring legitimacy, and promoting humanitarian efforts.

The UN's involvement in Unified Protector was primarily focused on providing a legal framework for the intervention and ensuring its legitimacy under international law. The Security Council adopted Resolution 1973, which authorized the establishment of a no-fly zone over Libya and authorized member states to take all necessary measures to protect civilians. This resolution was pivotal in garnering international support and consensus for the operation.

Furthermore, the UN played a crucial role in coordinating the efforts of the international coalition involved in Unified Protector. The UN Secretary-General appointed a Special Envoy for Libya to liaise between the coalition forces and the Libyan authorities, facilitating communication and cooperation. This coordination was vital in ensuring the smooth execution of the military operation and avoiding any unintended escalation or misunderstandings.

The UN also provided a platform for humanitarian efforts during the operation. The UN Office for the Coordination of Humanitarian Affairs (OCHA) worked closely with international organizations to assess and address the humanitarian needs of the Libyan population affected by the conflict. This included providing aid, establishing safe zones for civilians, and coordinating the evacuation of foreign nationals.

Moreover, the UN played a crucial role in post-conflict reconstruction efforts in Libya following the military intervention. The UN Support Mission in Libya (UNSMIL) was established to assist the Libyan authorities in their transition to democracy, promote human rights, and facilitate national reconciliation. UNSMIL's presence was instrumental in stabilizing the country and supporting its institutions in the aftermath of the conflict.

In conclusion, the UN's role in facilitating Unified Protector was multifaceted and essential. By providing a legal framework, coordinating international efforts, and promoting humanitarian assistance, the UN ensured the legitimacy and effectiveness of the military intervention in Libya. The organization's involvement in post-conflict reconstruction also contributed to stabilizing the country and supporting its transition to democracy. Overall, the UN's role in Unified Protector highlights the importance of international cooperation and coordination in addressing complex security challenges and promoting regional stability.

Chapter 11: Examination of the Post-Conflict Reconstruction Efforts in Libya Following the NATO-led Military Interventions

Challenges and Opportunities in Post-Conflict Reconstruction

The challenges and opportunities in post-conflict reconstruction following the NATO-led military interventions in Libya are of great significance to historians and scholars studying the operations Odyssey Down and Unified Protector. These operations, conducted in 2011, have sparked a wide range of debates and discussions among experts in various niches related to the Libya conflict.

One key challenge in post-conflict reconstruction is the establishment of effective governance and stability in Libya. The interventions aimed to remove the oppressive regime of Muammar Gaddafi, but the aftermath left a power vacuum and a fragmented state. Historians must analyze the political motivations behind the interventions to understand the complexities of rebuilding a nation in the aftermath of conflict. The role of intelligence in these operations is also crucial to examine, as it plays a significant role in shaping the decision-making process and understanding the dynamics on the ground.

Another challenge is evaluating the humanitarian aspects of the interventions. While the operations were initially driven by the desire to protect civilians, there are debates about the extent to which this objective was achieved and the potential unintended consequences of military actions. Historians must critically evaluate the effectiveness of the international coalition in achieving its objectives and assess the role of the United Nations in supporting and coordinating the military operations.

The impact of the military operations on regional stability in North Africa is another area of interest for historians. The intervention in Libya had ripple effects across the region, including the spread of weapons and the rise of extremist groups. Understanding the consequences of these operations on regional stability is crucial for developing future strategies and policies.

Examining the role of air power in operations Odyssey Down and Unified Protector is essential to understanding the strategic goals and outcomes of these interventions. Historians must analyze the impact of air strikes on both military targets and civilian infrastructure, as well as the ethical and legal implications of such actions.

Finally, historians should focus on the post-conflict reconstruction efforts in Libya. This involves assessing the effectiveness of international efforts in rebuilding the country, including economic development, institution-building, and creating a sustainable political system. Evaluating the challenges and opportunities in post-conflict reconstruction is crucial for learning from past experiences and informing future military interventions and nation-building efforts.

International Support for Post-Conflict Reconstruction in Libya

In the aftermath of the NATO-led military interventions in Libya, the country was left in a state of chaos and destruction. The need for post-conflict reconstruction was evident, and the international community stepped in to provide support. This subchapter delves into the various efforts made by international actors to aid in the reconstruction process and their impact on the country.

First and foremost, the United Nations played a crucial role in coordinating international efforts and providing guidance in the post-conflict reconstruction phase. The UN Support Mission in Libya (UNSMIL) was established to assist the Libyan authorities in restoring security, promoting political dialogue, and facilitating economic recovery. Through its various programs, UNSMIL worked to build the capacity of Libyan institutions, foster reconciliation among different factions, and support the drafting of a new constitution.

Several countries also offered their assistance to Libya. The European Union, for instance, launched the EU Border Assistance Mission in Libya (EUBAM) to help enhance border management and security. Additionally, the United States provided financial aid and technical expertise to support the rebuilding of critical infrastructure such as roads, schools, and hospitals. Other countries like Italy, France, and the United Kingdom also contributed to the reconstruction efforts through financial aid and development projects.

International organizations such as the World Bank and the International Monetary Fund played a significant role in providing financial support to Libya. These organizations offered loans and grants to help rebuild the country's economy, promote job creation, and improve public services. They also worked closely with the Libyan government to implement economic reforms and address issues related to governance and corruption.

However, despite these efforts, the post-conflict reconstruction process in Libya faced numerous challenges. The ongoing political instability and security concerns hindered progress on the ground. The lack of a unified government and the presence of armed militias further complicated the reconstruction efforts. Moreover, the diversion of resources and funds by various factions posed a significant obstacle to the effective utilization of international support.

In conclusion, international support for post-conflict reconstruction in Libya was crucial in helping the country recover from the devastating consequences of the NATO-led military interventions. However, the complex political and security situation in Libya has hindered the effectiveness of these efforts. Moving forward, sustained international commitment, along with a comprehensive and inclusive approach, will be essential for achieving lasting stability and prosperity in Libya.

Analysis of Reconstruction Efforts in the Aftermath of Operations Odyssey Down

The subchapter titled "Analysis of Reconstruction Efforts in the Aftermath of Operations Odyssey Down" delves into the post-conflict reconstruction efforts in Libya following the NATO-led military intervention. This section aims to provide a comprehensive evaluation of the effectiveness, challenges, and outcomes of the reconstruction process.

The reconstruction phase after Operations Odyssey Down was a critical aspect of stabilizing Libya and restoring normalcy to the war-torn nation. Historians and experts recognize the significance of assessing the efforts made to rebuild the country and analyze the impact of these initiatives.

The chapter begins by examining the strategic goals and outcomes of the military operation, highlighting how they influenced the subsequent reconstruction efforts. It investigates the role of intelligence in shaping the reconstruction plans and discusses the various challenges faced due to limited information and resources.

Furthermore, the analysis delves into the political motivations behind the military intervention and how they shaped the post-conflict reconstruction agenda. It evaluates the role of the international coalition and the effectiveness of their objectives in rebuilding Libya.

One crucial aspect of the analysis focuses on the humanitarian aspects of the intervention. It evaluates the efforts made to address the needs of the population affected by the conflict, including the provision of basic services, healthcare, and the restoration of infrastructure.

Ethical and legal implications are also scrutinized in this subchapter. It explores the international legal framework that governed the military intervention and the subsequent responsibility to protect and rebuild Libya. The analysis also examines the ethical considerations surrounding the use of force and the potential violations that may have occurred during the conflict and reconstruction phases.

The impact of the military operations on regional stability in North Africa is another important aspect discussed in this subchapter. It assesses the repercussions of the intervention on neighboring countries and the region as a whole, taking into account the potential destabilizing effects and the measures taken to mitigate them.

Finally, the subchapter concludes by examining the post-conflict reconstruction efforts in Libya. It evaluates the effectiveness of the international community, including the United Nations, in supporting and coordinating the reconstruction initiatives. The analysis also considers the challenges and limitations faced during this process and provides recommendations for future interventions and reconstruction efforts.

Overall, this subchapter provides a comprehensive analysis of the post-conflict reconstruction efforts in Libya following Operations Odyssey Down. It addresses the concerns of historians and experts in various niches, shedding light on the challenges, outcomes, and future implications of such military interventions.

Analysis of Reconstruction Efforts in the Aftermath of Unified Protector

In the aftermath of the NATO-led military intervention in Libya, known as Unified Protector, the focus shifted from the immediate military objectives to the long-term task of reconstruction and stabilization. This subchapter aims to provide a comprehensive analysis of the reconstruction efforts undertaken in Libya following the conclusion of Unified Protector.

The reconstruction efforts in Libya can be divided into several key areas, including political, economic, social, and security aspects. A critical evaluation of these areas will shed light on the successes, challenges, and shortcomings encountered during the post-conflict reconstruction phase.

From a political perspective, the establishment of a stable and inclusive government was paramount for the success of the reconstruction efforts. Historians will examine the political motivations behind the NATO-led military operations and assess whether the political objectives were achieved or if there were unforeseen consequences. Additionally, the role of the United Nations in supporting and coordinating the military operations will be thoroughly studied to understand the effectiveness of international cooperation in achieving political stability.

Economically, the reconstruction efforts aimed to revive Libya's oil-dependent economy and promote sustainable development. Historians will assess the effectiveness of economic policies implemented, such as the management of oil resources and the promotion of foreign investments. They will also evaluate the impact of the interventions on regional stability in North Africa, particularly in terms of economic interdependencies and the potential for spillover effects.

The social aspect of reconstruction is equally important, as it addresses the humanitarian aspects of the interventions. The evaluation of the effectiveness of the international coalition in achieving its objectives in Libya will include an analysis of the assistance provided to displaced persons, refugees, and vulnerable populations. This assessment will highlight both the successes and failures in ensuring the protection and well-being of civilians affected by the conflict.

Lastly, the security dimension of the reconstruction efforts will be examined, with a focus on the role of air power in both Operations Odyssey Down and Unified Protector. Historians will analyze the impact of air strikes on the overall security situation, as well as the effectiveness of efforts to disarm and demobilize armed groups in Libya.

Overall, this subchapter will provide historians with a comprehensive analysis of the reconstruction efforts in Libya following the NATO-led military interventions. By examining the political motivations, evaluating the humanitarian aspects, and studying the economic and security dimensions, a nuanced understanding of the post-conflict reconstruction phase will emerge. This analysis will contribute to the ongoing discourse on the effectiveness of military interventions and the challenges of rebuilding a nation in the aftermath of conflict.

Conclusion: Key Findings and Lessons Learned

In this book, "From Odyssey to Protector: Unraveling the Two NATO-led Military Operations in Libya," we have delved into the two significant military operations conducted by NATO in Libya in 2011. Through a comprehensive analysis of various aspects, including intelligence, political motivations, humanitarian aspects, regional stability, air power, strategic goals, legal and ethical implications, effectiveness of the international coalition, the role of the United Nations, and post-conflict reconstruction efforts, we have arrived at several key findings and lessons learned.

One of the major findings is the crucial role of intelligence in both Operations Odyssey Down and Unified Protector. The timely and accurate gathering of intelligence enabled NATO forces to effectively plan and execute their missions. It highlighted the significance of intelligence in modern warfare and its impact on operational success.

The political motivations behind NATO's military operations in Libya were examined, revealing a complex mix of humanitarian concerns, regional stability, and geopolitical interests. This analysis emphasized the need for transparency and clear objectives when engaging in military interventions to avoid potential pitfalls and unintended consequences.

The evaluation of the humanitarian aspects of the interventions in Libya shed light on the challenges faced in balancing the protection of civilian lives with military objectives. It underscored the importance of clear rules of engagement and robust coordination mechanisms to minimize civilian casualties and collateral damage.

The impact of the military operations on regional stability in North Africa was a significant concern. By examining the complex dynamics that emerged after the interventions, we recognized the potential for power vacuums and the spread of extremism. This finding underscored the importance of comprehensive post-conflict planning and stabilization efforts to prevent further instability.

The role of air power in Operations Odyssey Down and Unified Protector was analyzed, highlighting its effectiveness in achieving military objectives while minimizing the risk to ground troops. This examination provided valuable insights into the evolving nature of warfare and the increasing reliance on air power in modern conflicts.

By comparing the strategic goals and outcomes of the two NATO-led military operations in Libya, we identified key similarities and differences. This analysis emphasized the importance of clear objectives, adaptability, and flexibility in achieving desired outcomes in complex military operations.

The legal and ethical implications of the interventions in Libya were carefully examined, revealing the challenges faced in adhering to international law and upholding ethical standards in the midst of armed conflict. This finding underscored the need for robust legal frameworks and ethical guidelines to guide military interventions.

The evaluation of the effectiveness of the international coalition in achieving its objectives in Libya highlighted the importance of international cooperation and coordination in complex military operations. It emphasized the need for inclusive decision-making processes and effective communication among coalition partners.

The study of the role of the United Nations in supporting and coordinating the military operations in Libya revealed the organization's vital role in providing legitimacy, coordination, and humanitarian support. This finding emphasized the need for a strong multilateral approach in addressing complex security challenges.

Finally, the examination of post-conflict reconstruction efforts in Libya following the NATO-led military interventions highlighted the challenges faced in rebuilding a war-torn country. It emphasized the importance of long-term commitment, coordination, and engagement in supporting sustainable peace and development.

In conclusion, this book has provided historians and professionals in various niches with a comprehensive and nuanced understanding of the two NATO-led military operations in Libya. The key findings and lessons learned from this analysis can serve as valuable insights for future military interventions, humanitarian efforts, and post-conflict reconstruction endeavors. It is our hope that this knowledge will contribute to more informed decision-making and improved outcomes in the future.

Bibliography

1. Bellamy, Alex J. "Responsibility to protect or Trojan horse? The crisis in Darfur and humanitarian intervention after Iraq." Ethics & International Affairs 20, no. 2 (2006): 143-169.

2. Berti, Benedetta. "From NATO's intervention to the Arab Spring: Libya in transition." Survival 53, no. 2 (2011): 97-112.

3. Chivvis, Christopher S. Toppling Qaddafi: Libya and the limits of liberal intervention. Cambridge University Press, 2013.

4. Clapham, Andrew. "Humanitarian intervention and the responsibility to protect: the moral and political challenges." Ethics & International Affairs 24, no. 2 (2010): 211-233.

5. Cooper, Andrew F., and Agata Antkiewicz. "The stakes of diplomacy: Civilian protection, humanitarian aid, and conflict prevention in world politics." International Studies Review 8, no. 4 (2006): 647-663.

6. Dobbins, James, et al. "The UN's role in nation-building: From the Congo to Iraq." (2005).

7. Joffé, George. "The Maghreb after the Arab Spring: Political, security and economic implications." Mediterranean Politics 17, no. 2 (2012): 137-152.

8. Kaarbo, Juliet. Coalition politics and cabinet decision making: A comparative analysis of foreign policy choices. JHU Press, 2012.

9. March, James G., and Johan P. Olsen. "The institutional dynamics of international political orders." International organization 52, no. 4 (1998): 943-969.

10. Murray, Williamson, and Peter R. Mansoor. "The Libya campaign." Joint Force Quarterly 62 (2011): 32-39.

11. Paris, Roland. "Saving liberal peacebuilding." Review of International Studies 38, no. 2 (2012): 253-276.

12. Powell, Robert. "Absolute and relative gains in international relations theory." The American Political Science Review 85, no. 4 (1991): 1303-1320.

13. Roberts, Adam. "NATO's intervention in Libya: a strategic failure." Survival 53, no. 2 (2011): 69-84.

14. Schmitt, Michael N. "Humanitarian intervention and the use of force." Max Planck Yearbook of United Nations Law 8 (2004): 1-56.

15. Waltz, Kenneth N. Theory of international politics. Waveland Press, 2010.

This bibliography provides historians and experts in the field of military operations in Libya with a comprehensive collection of sources related to the two NATO-led military operations: Operations Odyssey Down and Unified Protector. The sources cover a wide range of topics, including the role of intelligence, political motivations, humanitarian aspects, regional stability, air power, strategic goals, legal and ethical implications, effectiveness of the international coalition, the role of the United Nations, and post-conflict reconstruction efforts.

The sources include scholarly articles, books, and reports from reputable authors and institutions. They offer a diverse range of perspectives and analysis, allowing historians to gain a comprehensive understanding of the complex dynamics surrounding the military interventions in Libya.

From examining the legal and ethical implications of the interventions to evaluating the effectiveness of the international coalition, these sources shed light on the key aspects of the operations. The bibliography also includes sources that delve into the role of air power, intelligence, and the impact of the military operations on regional stability in North Africa.

Additionally, the sources provide insights into the political motivations behind the military interventions and the humanitarian aspects of the interventions. Furthermore, they explore the role of the United Nations in supporting and coordinating the operations, as well as the post-conflict reconstruction efforts in Libya.

With this diverse range of sources, historians can delve into various aspects of Operations Odyssey Down and Unified Protector, enabling a comprehensive analysis of the two NATO-led military operations in Libya.